Green Living

How To Reduce Your Carbon Footprint

Table of Contents

Chapter 1

Introduction

Chapter 2

Recycling

Chapter 3

Save as Much Power as Possible

Chapter 4

Cut Back on the Use of Paper Products

Chapter 5

Transportation

Chapter 6

Organic Gardening & Lawn Care

Chapter 7

Additional Tips to Help you Live Green

Chapter 8

Conclusion

Chapter 1

Introduction

With all the information out there in the news and on the internet most people are at least aware of pollution problems. The issue is more serious in some areas but the fact remains that we all contribute to it. The concern is that with more people on Earth now and more pollution we are harming our environment.

Since we breath the air that is out there what is in it should be a top concern for each of us. Yet we often go about it without thinking twice about it. There are enough individuals suffering from health concerns due to what they have been breathing in for years.

With all of the pollutants out there right now, imagine what it will be like for future generations. You may don't care must as you won't be around. Yet you will have family who will need to deal with the problems. Even y our own children and grandchildren who are the next generations will be affected by it.

Each of us has the power to make some positive changes though. Some people believe that living green is a waste of time because you are only one person. Yet if the educational information out there about it could encourage many individuals to all do their part it would have quite a significant impact overall.

The efforts of only one person over the course of their lifetime will significantly reduce the amount of pollution out there. Teaching children from a young age what they can do and why will allow that process to continue being implemented in our society as well.

We also have the responsibility to let the government and businesses know that we expect them to take action. Buy what you can from companies that due have plenty of living green concepts incorporated for customers to take advantage of. At the same time you need to influence your government to place laws in effect that limit the amount of pollution that can be emitted by a company as well as by individual vehicles on the roads.

If you are ready to start living green and to do your part to reduce the carbon footprints you have placed on this Earth it is time to learn about the various ways you can do so. It is never too late to make some positive changes to your behaviors so that you can live healthier and so can everyone around you.

Chapter 2

Recycling

Recycling is one of the easiest as well as most effective ways that you can help the environment. There are plenty of different projects at home you can separate from your trash for this purpose. It is convenient if you buy plastic trash barrels and label them for individual products.

You should have one for glass, plastic, and cardboard. If you drink soda from cans then have one for those aluminum cans as well. Find out where you can take each of these full barrels to be recycled when you need to. There should be centers for them locally around town.

You will often find receptacles out there that allow you to place these items into at collection spots. They are just huge containers that will get emptied out on a regular basis. This is perfect when the community doesn't have any other method for taking in the items to be recycled.

If your community doesn't offer them you need to see what you can do to get them in place. You can contact your local officials in person or with a letter asking them to consider offering them. Explain your concerns that without such receptacles in place people won't be encouraged to recycle in your area.

The concept of recycling can extend to your schools and place of employment as well. Do your best to get this important issue recognized everywhere you can. In many instances people just need to be educated and then reminded about the benefits of recycling for our environment.

Your information can motivate them to take part in it. Don't overlook the importance of letting children know either. They are often very excited by recycling and find it to be thrilling. They can often help encourage their parents to take part in such efforts as well.

Buying products that have been recycled such as paper products is a great way to show your support for these efforts. You will notice some greeting cards are made from them. Even supplies such as napkins used in fast food restaurants can be made from recycled paper.

It is also very simple to carry around a large mesh bag when you are going to shop for a few items. Rather than getting a paper or plastic bag from them you can place your purchased items into your own bag. Look for one that is durable so it you can reuse it over and over again.

Chapter 3

Save as Much Power as Possible

We use electricity for many things in our lives, and often do so without thinking twice about it. We turn on the switch for lights in our home and to turn on electronic devices all the time. Yet we need to do our best to save as much power as we can.

The types of light bulbs that you are using can be a problem for the environment. There are many places that sell those that are energy efficient though. You can get them in any size you need for all the rooms in your home. They aren't very expensive and what you do spend on them you will save with a lower electricity bill each month.

It is very simple to cut back on the amount of lighting you use at all though. During the day open curtains and allow the natural sunlight to shine through. Then you will only need to turn on the lights at night when the sun goes down or on cloudy days.

The use of sky lights has become very popular for businesses and even in newer homes. This allows the sun to be shining through the ceiling and so less electricity has to be used. Some of the larger retail stores such as Wal-Mart use this as much as possible.

Look up as you walk through one of their stores. You will notice during the day they don't have very many lights on at all. Sometimes a cloud will roll in front of the sun and you will notice it immediately gets darker in the store than before. They are saving a huge amount of money on electricity and they are also helping the environment.

There are many ways in which you can generate electricity too that comes from alterative power. You can place solar panels on your roof which will collect electricity. That is the source your home will use for all of its needs when you turn the power on to something.

Should you run out of the solar power that has been collected it will immediately kick over to the regular electricity without any interruption to you at all. There is also the use of wind and water power in some areas. Take a look at these alternative methods and see what you can do with them for your own home.

A big waster of electricity that pollutes the environment is leaving light bulbs burning on your porch when you are away from home. You don't have to go without lighting when you return but you don't need to do it that way anymore. There are some great alternatives to consider.

You can place decorative solar lights along your driveway. Some of them are very short while others are tall lantern style. It is completely up to you which look you would like to have for the landscaping of your home. Since you don't need to plug them in to an outlet you can place them anywhere you would like to out there.

These lights collect power from the sun in the day time and as soon as it gets dark they will illuminate your hard. When they run out of solar power they will turn off. Should they have enough to last all night then they will turn off when they sun comes up and start collecting energy to use all over again.

Another alternative is to install a motion light. This is a type that doesn't have to be left on when you leave home. When you pull into your driveway it will turn on based on the movement it has detected. It will remain on for a short period of time which allows you to get safely into your home with the light you need.

The use of windmills in many areas to create energy is also being looked at. Sometimes water known as hydropower is available too. However, the light bulbs you use can help you get the most out of these benefits.

If from start to finish everything in your electricity gathering and using process is eco-friendly you won't feel bad about consuming it to operate lights and the electronics that you use in your home and business.

Chapter 4
Cut Back on the Use of Paper Products

Paper products are used all the time in our society, and that means more trees are being cut down to keep up with that demand. The trees live off the carbon dioxide that is in the air we breath. As their numbers are depleted, there will be more carbon dioxide remaining in the oxygen we breathe.

There are many ways in which you can cut back on the use of paper both at home and at work. If you get a ton of junk mail each week it can become a chore to weed through all of it. Go online and sign up to opt out of receiving it that way the amount of paper waste in your home will be reduced by about 1/3 without you having to do much about it.

Find out which of your accounts you can get an online statement for. This way you further reduce the amount of paper that comes your way. Log on each month and find out what you owe as well as checking over your statements. If necessary print what information you do need instead of the entire statement.

You can also pay bills online which will save paper in the areas of checks and envelopes. It only takes a few minutes to set up such accounts and then you can do the process each month. If you don't want to mess with that each month then have the bills taken directly out of your checking account. The fact that this is so convenient is also a terrific benefit that you will certainly want to take advantage of

Try to buy notebooks, greeting cards, and other products that you see have been made from recycled paper. You can even use napkins and paper towels that have been recycled. Keeping clothes in your kitchen though is often a great saver of paper towels.

Encourage everyone at your office to cut back on the use of paper when they can. In fact, you should talk to your boss about implementing some effective ideas. For example there can be a pile for waste paper that everyone can use for various needs. The back sides can be used to take down phone messages and other correspondence that doesn't have to look professional.

With reports, make sure information is printed on both sides of the paper. It will still look very professional and it will cut the amount of paper used for the process in half. It is important to double check the information you plan to print as well first so you don't view it, see a mistake, and then have to print it again.

Chapter 5

Transportation

With more vehicles on the road today than ever before transportation is a huge factor with pollution. Even with emissions laws in place that limit how much pollution a car can give out, the accumulative amount of it is unbelievable. Taking the time to do your part to cut down on it will ensure everyone is healthier and breathing cleaner air.

You may be saying that you have to use your car to get around so you aren't going to read this section. It is agreed that being able to hop in your own car and go where you wish is important. However, it is also important that you understand there are still changes that can be made to reduce the amount of emissions that take place when you do.

Many of us are very attached to our vehicle as we see it to be a life line that keeps us going where we want to be. It is convenient to have your own vehicle and it offers you a way to get to work, take care of your errands, and to do leisurely activities that you enjoy.

It is important to take proper care of your vehicle to reduce pollution. If you have a damaged exhaust system or other problem you need to get it resolved right away. You can get a complete diagnosis for it from your local mechanic. Some people are able to fix such problems on their own and that is fine too.

Even though you do need your vehicle, you may be able to use it less. Can you walk to the store or the park? Can you carpool for work or to get the kids to their various activities? This will reduce the number of vehicles on the road each day by doing so.

Place a message on the bulletin board in the work lunch room, at your child's dance class, and other such locations. This will be to inform other driver's that you are interested in carpooling. In order for it to work though everyone involved must be committed to being ready on time and to driving at their specified times.

There are also modes of public transportation in many areas. You can commute by taking a bus, subway, or a train that many other people are on. This will save you the wear and tear on your vehicle as well. With the cost of gas these days it can prove to be more affordable for you as well. If you have a lengthy commute you can also use that time to get some work done both directions or to enjoy a good book.

There are some very good vehicles on the market that have been recognized as being environmentally friendly. Honda is a leader in this area the Civic. They also have a hybrid model which we will talk more about in a moment. They Toyota Prius is also variable in a standard or hybrid model. This is one of the top selling hybrid vehicles in the world.

There are some compact cars that are very eco-friendly and at the same time you can save money on fuel. If you can by comfortable with your lifestyle in a compact vehicle then check out the Mini Cooper, Ford Focus, and Honda Fit. Knowing that the vehicle you are driving is very environmentally friendly should make you feel good each time you drive it.

The hybrid models are those that have an alternate fuel source in addition to gas. They either operate with the use of electricity or solar power. This is the fuel source that is used first before any gas is accessed. When those sources are depleted then the vehicle switches to gas.

As soon as you recharge the main energy source the use of gas is stopped and it goes back to that alternative. Even when you are relying upon the gas for power though it is going to burn in a way that is very good for the environment. Hybrids can be quite expensive though so even with so much to offer many consumers have to pass them up.

Chapter 6

Organic Gardening & Lawn Care

Taking care of our home inside and out is something most of us do take plenty of pride in. We want to be able to make it the very best that it can be. The landscaping outside is what everyone who drives by and who stops to visit us will see. It is important to use to be able to arrive home and to feel welcomed there by what we see.

In order to get your garden and your grass to look its very best though you need to have the right tools and the right ingredients. Too many people assume this means you use pesticides and other chemicals to kill weeds and to keep pests out. Yet you can have a lovely garden and lawn organically so you won't be harming the environment in the process.

Fertilizer for your grass has a great deal of chemicals in it. The two main chemicals found in them that are problematic are nitrates and phosphates. Since it takes several pounds of fertilizer to complete one yard you will be exposing your family and pets to unnecessary problems.

You may not realize it but the use of such fertilizers can trigger asthma, be linked to cancers, and even cause neurological problems for your pets and young children. These chemicals also get into the soil and then run downstream into water supplies.

Instead of using this switch to natural compost. You can buy it or you can even make your own. The process of making your own isn't very difficult at all. You simply get a compost container and you place food scraps, the droppings from your pets, and even the leaves from your yard into the container.

This will become the compost you get the nutrients from for your lawn and your garden. You want to save your materials all year long to make enough compost. This is because the amount you end up with will be significantly compact compared to the volume of materials that you start out with.

With healthy soil to place your grass seed on, it will be able to grow much healthier. It will have longer roots which ensures survival. At the same time you will need to offer it less water to stay green. This is going to help you cut back on your water bill as well.

With many areas being on water restriction in the summer months, you want to be able to get as much use out of it as possible. By having the soil properly prepared you can still have a lovely green lawn even when you are restrained to only allocating water for certain periods of time on specific days of the week.

To get the most out of the water you put on your grass you need to take care of it in the early morning hours. This will result in more of it getting into the soil and less being lost to the process of evaporation. Many individuals believe that they can get the same results if they water at night. However, a big problem is that this leaves your grass very susceptible to various types of fungus growing.

To ensure your garden is able to benefit from the water you provide keep the ground level. You don't want it to all run off and therefore not offer the items in your garden the water they need to thrive. A good option to think about is to place mulch in a nice layer over the top of the soil. This will prevent the water from evaporating so your plants and flowers will get to retain more of it.

If you plan to spend a great deal of time enjoying the grass you have grown you want to do so organically. This way your family won't be at risk of anything. Look for type of grass that tends to grow well in your area. Not all of them are universal so selecting the wrong one can result in you being disappointed with the overall look of your lawn.

You also want a grass that is going to hold up well to people walking on it and playing on it. You don't want to have to keep everyone off of your lawn in order for it to continue looking nice. This can be a sad outlook because it will be inviting, especially under the shade trees and not being able to go out there isn't going to make your family happy.

Some individuals immediately reach for chemicals to kill off weeds that grown in their garden or their lawn. Yet this isn't the right solution to turn to. First, find out what type of weeds you are growing. That will tell you what the problem may be in that area. Some weeds are actually good for your lawn and you will want to leave them.

They can serve as a natural fertilizer for your yard. The rest of them you want to pull out by hand or to use tools to remove them. Make sure you get them from the roots up so they can't regrow as easily.

It is often a thought to just run them over with a mower and be done with them but avoid doing so. There are seeds in the weeds and when you do this they will spread all over the place. That will result in your lawn having more weeds than before and in various locations spread throughout it.

You may want to consider getting a different type of lawn mower too. Those that operate with the use of gas are placing pollutants into the air. If you have a very small lawn you may want to consider using a reel type.

These are hand propelled and use sharp blades underneath to cut the grass. You can adjust the blades to accommodate how short you wish to cut the grass. They are very simple to use and don't make much noise.

That means you can be out there using this type of lawn mower any time of the day or day of the week without bothering your neighbors. You will also get some exercise as you walk around the yard cutting it. You can find a quality reel lawn mower for about $40 - $60.

If you don't want to put your strength into using a reel mover you can look for an electric one. Many of the older models required you to use an extension cord to get a power supply though.

That was often annoying as you had to continually move the long cord out of your way as you moved along cutting the grass. Many heavy duty extension cords were lost in this process due to being ran over by the sharp blades of the lawn mower.

You will find that some significant improvements have been made to this type of lawn mower. Instead of using a cord to get the power source there is a small battery that provides it. They are extremely quite and that helps with noise pollution as well.

There are many models and sizes of electric lawn mowers that you can find out there. They range in price from $125 to $600 depending on how much power you want and what size you wish to buy. Take a look around to see what is going to be the perfect match for your own lawn care needs.

Chapter 7
Additional Tips to Help you Live Green

There are plenty of small areas where you can make some significant changes as well. The concepts here are very easy and anyone can implement then to start living greener right now. You will be proud to offer such benefits to the environment without having to give up anything you really need.

It is important to drink plenty of water each day. Yet you often see people carrying around plastic bottles of it. In many instances bottled water doesn't taste any better than the tap water but manufacturers of bottled water want you to think there is.

Instead of getting a new bottle each time you drink water get some reusable containers. You can fill them up with water and even ice if you prefer and drink them everywhere you go. There are several sizes, colors, and designs that you can choose from. This process will significantly reduce the amount of plastic that is in our environment.

If you do live in an area where it isn't safe to drink the tap water then you want to make sure you recycle those plastic bottles. That way they don't end up in landfills. You can also get bottled water delivered to your home in large containers.

Then you can just fill up your own water bottles that you reuse from there. That is a great way to get healthy water and to eliminate waste at the same time. You will also find that getting bottled water this way is cheaper than buying those individual bottles at the store and from the vending machines.

When you complete projects in your home such as remodeling and painting you will likely have left over supplies. You aren't going to be able to do much with most of them. Paint is a substance that you don't want to place at landfills due to the chemicals found in them. They can get underground and do a great deal of damage. A better alternative is to donate that left over paint and supplies.

There are many organizations that collect such items to help others. This can be Church groups, community organizations, and specific programs so find out what is available in your area. You can even search online to find out how to donate such items to a worthy cause.

The left over paint can be mixed with many others that people have donated. It can be used to paint houses, paint schools, and to make your town look nicer by reducing fences and such. This is a great way to prevent those leftovers from being wasted and from harming the environment.

Make sure you properly dispose of pollutants that can be very dangerous for the Earth. It is common for people to change their oil at home to save money and to get the job done quickly. Never pour that oil on the ground as it will get into the soil. This is going to erode the ground of essential nutrients necessary in order for something to grow there.

When oil gets into the water it can result in aquatic life dying. This is very serious as it will upset the balance of the natural food chain. It can result in problems in that part of the water decades after it has taken place. It is also possible for the oil to get into drinking water if you aren't careful.

We have all heard plenty of information about the warnings of skin cancer from being in the sun without proper sunscreen. What we often don't realize though is that what is in that sunscreen can be polluting both the water and the air around us.

You want to avoid using chemical sunscreens as they aren't good for the environment. They aren't going to offer you any more protection than those made from titanium oxide or zinc oxide. Read the labels on the sunscreen products you purchase and make sure you get a high enough SPF that is right for your skin.

There are plenty of aerosol cans of sunscreen out there and you want to avoid using them as well. These types of dispensers can be very harmful to the ozone layers. Instead choose one you can spray on your body with a spray bottle nozzle or that you can dispense like a lotion and spray on your body.

Sunscreen isn't the only type of aerosol that you should avoid though. Look for products to clean your home and even hairspray that isn't going to be harming the environment. There are alternative dispensing sources to them so you aren't limited to relying on anything in an aerosol form.

Chapter 8

Conclusion

Living Green is something we should all be concerned about. Making the world a better place for us and for future generations is very important. The damages we do today will have a significant impact on the rest of the world. Young children, adults, and even the elderly can all get involved in making the world a better place for all of us.

In the past decade there has been more information and education on this subject offered than ever before. Various types of organizations including the government, Boy Scouts, Girl Scouts, the Environmental Protection Agency, and others have been attempting to share all they can about the concerns for our environment as well as ways to help.

There are plenty of celebrities involved in living green projects as well. Actors, musicians, and other prestigious figures tend to have quite a following around the world. People listen to what they have to say and therefore such public service announcements have proven to be extremely effective.

As a result more manufactures of products we use everyday are getting involved as well. They are offering more products that are safe for the environment and that offer you plenty of benefits. You can encourage other companies to follow their example by not buying them if they aren't safe for the environment.

If they are losing sales they will find out why and make important changes to get those customers back. The demands of the consumer are extremely powerful and they will be able to generate a positive response from our manufacturers. As a result everyone wins and we will have a safer environment to live in. If you continue to buy what they are offering now though they won't have the encouragement they need to take saving the environment seriously.

The amount of trash that the common household tosses out each day is unbelievable. It isn't unusual for that to be at least on bag per day when all is said and done. All of that waste ends up at our landfills and just what comes from your household alone adds up to quite a bit over the course of a year.

Remove what you can from that trash and recycle it. This can be paper products, glass, plastic, and cardboard. You will be surprised at just how much of this you can separate and recycle. If you have a trash bin for each of them in the garage or in your backyard then it will be much easier to stay on task with this type of effort.

Be conscious of the paper products you are using as well. That way you can use some alternatives. For example cloth napkins instead of disposable ones are a great idea for a restaurant. Use both sides of paper so that you can reduce the amount of it that you use by 50%.

Take papers you don't need and cut them into squares. You can create your own notepads this way for phone messages, quick family notes, and to write your grocery list or errands on. You can cut back paper by eliminating unnecessary mail as well.

We live in an electronic age due to technology and all of the advances that have come along with it. Yet from various types of light bulbs and sources there is damage being done to the environment. By changing the types that use to the more energy efficient ones on the market you can save money on your electric bill and help protect the environment.

Don't forget to look into alternative sources of energy that will allow you to not use electricity as often. One of the easiest to implement for any home or business is the use of solar power. In some areas wind and water power are also available.

How you get around is one of the biggest areas where you can make a difference for the environment. The amount of pollutants that are emitted each day from vehicles is very high. Do all you can to make sure your vehicles are in compliance with the laws. Only use them when you need to so that you cut down on driving time.

Combine your activities so you can eliminate trips to town as well. Do your best to set up carpools or to access public transportation when available. If you are in the market for a new vehicle consider one that has been recognized as being environmentally friendly. There are many great ones to choose from so you won't be limited in size or style.

You can also go with the hybrid models which will save you money on gas, they aren't going to harm the environment, and they will need less routine maintenance. A hybrid is a very solid investment and something you will be extremely proud to drive. It shows that you do care about the environment in many ways.

There are several great hybrid vehicles out there right now. Most of them are compact and medium sized vehicles. However, for 2009 you will find more larger cars, a minivan, and even some full sized pickups emerging. This is due to the consumer demands for such vehicles as a hybrid. The manufacturers out there are listening so keep letting them know what your interested in.

Home is where the heart is and a place you want to be harm and inviting. Establishing a very beautiful lawn and garden is part of that image. You can accomplish your desire to have them without harming your family, pets, or the environment. Don't use any types of chemicals as they have been linked to many ill effects you want to avoid.

Organic lawn care and gardening isn't difficult it just takes a different approach. If you go about it the right way it will cost you less to get your lawn and garden ready each year too. You will be relying up natural items around your home and yard for the compost which will reduce the amount of your trash that ends up at the landfill.

A healthy lawn is one that is well cared for, and you can see yours thrive when you remove the chemicals from the equation. You can also look at environmentally friendly lawn mowers that won't cause you to pollute the environment each time you turn them on.

You will feel great seeing the results of your efforts. At the same time you will know you know you are offering your friends and family a very safe lawn to play and relax on with you. That is a feeling that you will be very proud of even if no one around you has a clue why you are smiling from ear to ear.

There are plenty of tips and strategies offered in order to help us have an environment that is less polluted. It doesn't take a great deal of time or effort in order to be a part of most of them. You simply have to be committed to being a part of the solution instead of the problem.

Continue to do your part by making changes where you can. Get your entire family involved and explain to them why it is so important. Share your views with friends and family members as well. They may not realize the importance of their efforts.

Once you enlighten them you will be able to encourage them in their efforts. In most regards individuals aren't out there destroying the environment on purpose. It is often a lack of information or not feeling like they can really make a difference that leads to it.

If you find that a person or a business is polluting the environment with chemicals or other substances intentionally then you need to report it. This could be your neighbor or even the company that they work for. No one needs to know you are the person responsible for reporting it.

You can make a report with your local law enforcement or with your local health department. They will do an inspection and handle the situation based on what they find. There are laws in place to prevent this type of blatant disregard for the environment. Those found guilty of doing so can be fined, have to pay the cost of cleaning it up, and even face criminal charges that can result in jail time.

It is possible to live green and to reduce your carbon footprints on the environment. It is understandable why you want to leave a legacy behind you but do it in a positive manner. Each person has the choice of how they will live their life. Be proud of the efforts you make to keep our world in as good of shape as you possible can.

The rewards of doing so will come back to you as well as future generations. We all have the power and the ability to change what we are doing now in exchange for better ways of living. Decide now you want to modify your behaviors and feel good about your lifestyle choices. It doesn't matter how long you have been doing things the other way.

Every bit of change that takes place out there is going to make a positive difference overall. Be a part of finding the solution for a better environment to live in. This will benefit your health as well as that of your children. Such efforts are definitely worth it in order to reap these types of rewards.

One person and one voice can unite with many more to create a significant effect that shows how much people care about the world in which they live in. Do all you can to make these efforts a part of your world. Pass them on to your children so the benefits can continue for them and their generation as well.

Green Living Tips